NEW VANGUARD 217

# BRITISH LIGHT TANKS 1927–45

Marks I–VI

**DAVID FLETCHER**        ILLUSTRATED BY HENRY MORSHEAD

First published in Great Britain in 2014 by Osprey Publishing,
PO Box 883, Oxford, OX1 9PL, UK
PO Box 3985, New York, NY 10185-3985, USA
E-mail: info@ospreypublishing.com

Osprey Publishing is part of the Osprey Group

A CIP catalogue record for this book is available from the British Library

Print ISBN: 978 1 78200 377 9
PDF ebook ISBN: 978 1 78200 378 6
ePub ebook ISBN: 978 1 78200 379 3

Index by Zoe Ross
Typeset in Sabon and Myriad Pro
Originated by PDQ Media, Bungay, UK
Printed in China through Worldprint Ltd

14 15 16 17 18   10 9 8 7 6 5 4 3 2 1

Osprey Publishing is supporting the Woodland Trust, the UK's leading
woodland conservation charity, by funding the dedication of trees.

**www.ospreypublishing.com**

# CONTENTS

# BRITISH LIGHT TANKS 1927–45

## MARKS I–VI

### INTRODUCTION

There is one British tank that fought in virtually every tank battle involving British armour from the outbreak of World War II until 1941 but which rarely, if ever, gets a mention in any modern accounts. The tank in question is the Light Tank Mark VI, specifically the VIB and VIC.

They operated in France with the British Expeditionary Force (and would have fought in Norway if the ship carrying them had not been sunk), in the Western Desert, in Italian East Africa, in Greece with the 4th Hussars, in Malta, in Cyprus and in Syria with the Australians. They served in Iran with the 14th/20th Hussars, in India they operated with British and Indian regiments on the North-West Frontier and a few, formed as a light-tank company, were rushed to Singapore in December 1941 in a vain effort to stem the Japanese advance through Malaya. Meanwhile, B Squadron, 3rd Hussars, detached from its regiment in the Middle East, was sent by sea to Singapore. The Japanese scuppered that plan, and after a short spell on Sumatra the squadron landed in Java. However, it was once again too late, and ended up destroying its tanks and surrendering.

In addition to India, both Australia and Canada received deliveries of variants of the Light Tank Mark VI, particularly for training purposes. In both countries they were also available for home defence, should the need ever arise, as indeed they were in Great Britain. They were even used by the Germans; an officer named Becker acquired many captured tanks and converted them into an impressive range of small, self-propelled guns, as well as supply and command vehicles. There are enough stories here to fill a fair-sized book, although for the present we are limited to one slim volume.

Of course, before the Mark VI there were other types, including some interesting prototypes. They played a significant part in the story of the mechanisation of the British Army.

### PROTOTYPES AND PREDECESSORS

If we ignore one strange machine with a turret at each end built by Royal Ordnance in 1924, sometimes referred to as the three-man light tank and sometimes as a machine-gun carrier, the first light tank proper to come to the notice of the British Army was the Carden-Loyd Mark VII, which was shown in a War Office booklet published in 1930. It was built by Vickers-Carden-Loyd Ltd in 1928 and displays its Carden-Loyd lineage in the suspension system. The booklet says that it was the first light tank with a revolving turret, although that is questionable, and it goes on to say that it 'has considerable mechanical defects but showed great promise'. If what evolved from it is any guide then that is quite true, although looking at it one feels that it must also have been terribly cramped inside, even for a two-man crew.

The original Light Tank A4E1 seen outside the hangars at Farnborough and photographed from the rear. The suspension features the external beam, typical of the earlier Carden-Loyd carriers. The shallow machine-gun turret would have been very cramped.

In September 1928 a contract was signed for a further four tanks from Vickers-Carden-Loyd, which were designated the Light Tank Mark I. The publication mentioned above had this to say about them: 'A vastly better fighting machine. The turret is geared and mechanically great improvements have been made. This Light Tank is considered sufficiently satisfactory to put into the Service. Messrs. Vickers Armstrong [sic] are responsible for the design.'

The mechanical improvements are not specified, but the engine, a Meadows type EOC straight six, was said to be 'improved', although it could only deliver the same 59bhp as its predecessor. Other sources mention a two-plus-two gearbox, presumably like the original Carden-Loyd system, and tiller steering. The most obvious mechanical improvement has to be the suspension. Vickers moved away from the Carden-Loyd arrangement, with the external, horizontal bar, and opted instead for a Horstmann design in which pairs of spoked road wheels were linked by a cast bracket and a quarter-elliptical leaf spring. It undoubtedly gave a rough ride, but much better was to come. The hull shape was improved and, although a crew of two was retained, the men now had more headroom. There was a raised cover for the driver to use and the turret was a good deal taller than the first

This photograph shows A4E5 (T494 ML8787) on a raft being ferried across what is assumed to be the Basingstoke Canal. The tank has its turret reversed and appears to be camouflage painted. It also features what appears to be a revised suspension with horizontal coil springs.

type. Whether, as the book claims, it could mount a .50-cal machine gun as an alternative to the .303-cal appears to be doubtful, but the fact that the turret was 'geared' is interesting. It was traversed by turning a handle, which then turned a gear wheel that meshed with a toothed turret ring.

All four tanks went to the Mechanical Warfare Experimental Establishment (MWEE) in October 1929 and remained there until early 1933. Three of them appear to have been identical, but the fourth, A4E2, was supplied with a twin .50-cal anti-aircraft mount, using a pair of Vickers heavy, water-cooled machine guns. It was a mounting that the company seemed keen to promote, since it was also seen on a prototype Crossley 6x4 armoured car. Figures quoted by MWEE for all four tanks give a maximum armour thickness of 14mm, a weight of around 3.25 tonnes and a maximum road speed of 35 miles per hour.

By the time these tanks were released from MWEE in 1933 they were clearly obsolete, but since they were regarded only as prototypes they are unlikely to have entered service in the sense of being issued to actual Royal Tank Corps battalions. There may have been trips down to Bovington and Lulworth for mechanical and gunnery trials, and one was certainly used at a military display where it was rafted across a river, but all, presumably, under the auspices of MWEE.

Meanwhile a further five tanks were ordered from Vickers-Carden-Loyd Ltd and delivered to MWEE in 1930. They were classified by the manufacturer as the Carden-Loyd Mark VIII, although they were known to the War Office as the Light Tank Mark IA. Like the Mark I they were still only prototypes, and although two of them were issued briefly to 5th Battalion, Royal Tank Corps at Tidworth on Salisbury Plain, they were mostly used as trial vehicles to try out improved suspension systems or (in two cases) different engines and transmission, in particular a Ricardo S65 diesel engine and a Dorman gearbox. One was sent out for trials in the Middle East.

The most interesting of these vehicles was the fifth, A4E10, which had a special, tall turret that mounted two machine guns, one above the other, and seems to have spent much of its time at Lulworth. Otherwise, the new tanks were similar to the first batch but with higher sloped sides on the hull, which created more headroom for the crew, although in order to keep the weight down, armour thickness was reduced from 14mm to 9mm, offset to some extent by the use of sloped plates.

Four of these tanks were also built for trials in India. They all appear to have had the second type of suspension, designed by Horstmann, and they all seem to have performed very well. Following trials at Chaklala they embarked upon a 270-mile road trip to Razmak, deep in the North-West Frontier territory. They completed this as part of a convoy of wheeled vehicles, with which they were able to keep pace. At Razmak they were tested in the mountains, climbing steep scree slopes and coping well with snow, much to the dismay of local tribesmen who were more used to the road-bound armoured cars. They can be readily identified by the extra ventilation panels on the right side, above the engine, and were also used to test various designs of turret cupola that commanders found useful when under fire in the passes.

One thing that plagued this entire family of tanks was the springiness of the suspension, which made accurate firing on the move almost impossible. Of course, it made for excellent performance both on and off the road, but in an era when firing on the move was part of the whole raison d'être of Royal Tank Corps policy this was regarded as quite a handicap, as indeed was the vehicle's tendency to throw a track. This may explain the logic behind another unusual light tank, which appeared in 1930. It was a peculiar thing, and the whole point appears to have been to create a tank with a suspension stiff enough to make it capable of firing on the move. The suspension, which has a rather stolid appearance including short, limited deflection leaf springs, cannot have made for such a smooth ride. Later it is reported to have been fitted with a Horstmann-type suspension, but no photograph of this has yet been found. Despite its hefty appearance it weighed less than 5 tons and had a respectable top speed of 28mph, and although the design was never repeated it was the first three-man light tank, armed with a pair of machine guns in what was described as a Lanchester-type turret.

## LIGHT TANK MARK II

Now that the trial period was over it was time to begin building production tanks for service use, and an initial order for 16 was placed in December 1930. A total of 12 would come from Vickers-Armstrongs while the remaining four would come from the government's own Royal Ordnance Factory. There is nothing to distinguish them, and the only way to tell them apart is by their War Department or civil registration numbers; although they are easily distinguished from their predecessors, the Mark IA, by the shape of the turret. Designed by the Royal Ordnance Factory, this was rectangular

Only two of the amphibious light tanks were tested in British Army service. This is the second of them, T986, photographed outside the hangars at Farnborough. These tanks had the cowled propeller, instead of the separate rudder arrangement seen on some commercial examples.

in plan view, with sloped sides and rear. Much larger than the rounded turret on the Mark IA, it was still only intended for one man but, in addition to the Vickers machine-gun mounting at the front, it had sufficient space in the rear for a No 1 Wireless set, assuming one was available.

### 1: LIGHT TANK MARK I AT FARNBOROUGH

The Mechanical Warfare Experimental Establishment (MWEE) was set up at Pinewood Barracks, Farnborough, to examine and evaluate all new military vehicles for the British Army. This tank, MWEE number 189b, was one of four prototypes designed by Vickers-Armstrongs Ltd, which arrived there in October 1929. Three of them were more or less identical although the fourth featured a special anti-aircraft turret equipped with two heavy machine guns.

Given the General Staff specification A4E4 this particular light tank appeared in a lavish booklet entitled *Demonstration of Progress in the Mechanization in the Army since November 1926* where it was described as 'considered sufficiently satisfactory to be put into the Service'. By that time some of these tanks had done some limited work with Regular Army service units – often 2nd Battalion, Royal Tank Corps since it was located in the same area. It was a two-man tank, somewhat cramped inside, particularly in the turret, armed with a single Vickers machine gun. Small, fast and relatively cheap it suited the defence budget of that time and was seen as a vehicle for reconnaissance and liaison. Not perhaps a fighting tank except in colonial warfare situations, but quite good for the time, its successors make an interesting study.

### 2. LIGHT TANK MARK IIB, 6th AUSTRALIAN CAVALRY REGIMENT, EGYPT 1940

The Light Tank Mark II series was getting a bit long in the tooth by 1940, having been built in 1930–31. However they, with an assortment of Universal Carriers, were all that were available to equip the Australians when they arrived in the Middle East in 1940. In October 1940 the Australian 6th Divisional Cavalry Regiment was issued with six of these light tanks, described as 'very well used', to supplement their Carriers. The tanks were painted in the angular camouflage scheme, known as the Caunter Pattern after Brigadier J. A. L. 'Blood' Caunter who devised it. The tanks were even older than those the regiment had trained on in Australia, although the latter were few in number and only available briefly for initial training.

The Light Tank Mark IIB was a two-man machine with an enlarged turret, powered by a Rolls-Royce six-cylinder engine and quite fast enough in its day, but poorly armoured and prone to break down unless nursed very carefully. However, since they were all that was available to begin with they had to do, although when they went into action the Australians preferred to use the Carriers than the light tanks, which were both few in number and unreliable. Subsequently the regiment's A Squadron, then serving as part of the Western Desert Force, was partially equipped with captured Italian medium tanks for the attack on Tobruk. These tanks had been captured in large numbers during the battle of Beda Fomm in February 1941.

1

2

A column of light tanks moving carefully through a country town. The leading tank is a Vickers-Armstrongs-built Light Tank Mark IIB, identified by the petrol filler cap on the side, although in this case the registration number gives it away.

Another improvement was less obvious. This was the adoption of Cemented Tank Armour, or CTA plate, which in modern terms would be described as face-hardened armour, reckoned to be about 20 per cent more effective in terms of resistance to armour-piercing projectiles than conventional homogeneous armour. This meant that thinner plates could be used, which in turn offered a reduction in overall weight. CTA plate was adopted for all future types of light tank up to the Mark VI.

In mechanical terms the Mark II followed previous practice, although it was appreciated that something better was required. Thus the engine, a six-cylinder, water-cooled Meadows type EPC, was installed, offset to the right, driving through a two-speed and reverse primary gearbox via a two-speed epicyclic box to the front-mounted driving axle. There was a further reduction at each end of the driving axle and simple clutch-and-brake steering, operated by a tiller bar. This did not prove popular with drivers since it could result in the worrying experience known as reverse steering. As a result it was decided to replace the original transmission with a new one incorporating the Wilson pre-selective gearbox and twin lever steering.

In order to fulfil the requirement that each of three Royal Tank Corps battalions, described as mixed battalions, should include 22 light tanks, the War Office agreed to order a further 50. Production would be shared between the Royal Ordnance Factory, who would build 29 designated as Mark IIA, while Vickers-Armstrongs received a contract for 21 identified as Mark IIB. It is interesting, in passing, to note that this total of 66 tanks of the Light Tank Mark II type was exactly what was required to complete the three mixed battalions. There was no provision at all for spare or reserve tanks. Both Marks IIA and IIB featured the new transmission from the outset.

It is virtually impossible to distinguish a Mark IIA from a Mark IIB. A filler cap on the left side of the IIB is a clue, but only if you can see the left side, otherwise the WD or registration number is the only indication. A Mark IIA had two fuel tanks whereas a Mark IIB had one, albeit of a greater capacity than the two in the Mark IIA. However, it was possible to distinguish between the original Mark II and its successors. Marks IIA and IIB had an armoured flap at the front of the hull, to the right of the driver, and on both sides of the turret a protected ventilation louvre ran along the top edge, which shows up as a strip of armour standing proud from the turret on each side.

The fact that 66 of these tanks had been built with the intention of completing three Royal Tank Corps battalions with their complement of light tanks may not have been honoured to the full, since some of them were clearly earmarked for experimental purposes. In 1932 when the need for more power was deemed desirable, the Meadows engines were removed and replaced by the Rolls-Royce 20/25bhp type.

Trials on the Indian Frontier with the Mark IA light tanks as reported in the *Royal Tank Corps Journal* seemed very favourable. A series of articles by three RTC officers, Colonel Studd, Major Kenchington and Major Birks had made the case for light tanks in India instead of armoured cars on the grounds that they could travel more widely in that region, and the authorities seemed disposed to agree; a number of armoured-car companies were redesignated light-tank companies and equipped with the Light Tank Mark IIB Indian Pattern, a modified version of the British type. Although somewhat light on armour since it was only likely to come under rifle fire, the Mark IIB had an extra stowage locker at the rear, a protected cupola for the commander on top of the turret and cooling louvres covering the engine compartment on the offside. The Indian light tanks had the same engine, transmission and suspension as their British counterparts but did not go through the process of replacing the Meadows engine with the Rolls-Royce unit. Exactly how many were supplied is not clear, but it seems to have been for a minimum of three companies, which with 16 tanks apiece works out at 48 tanks, so the minimum figure must have been about 50. One entry in a Vickers-Armstrongs ledger quotes either 54 or 59, which is probably about right.

Hopefully this is a joke. One reluctant mule is harnessed to an Indian Pattern Light Tank Mark IIB to help it over a rough bit of ground. In real life one mule would not be strong enough to move a light tank, not even with two men pushing. Notice the turret cupola, characteristic of light tanks in India.

# LIGHT TANK MARK III

The Light Tank Mark III gets short shrift in most published works on tanks, as it was little more than a production version of the improved Light Tank Mark IIB, with the new suspension, Rolls-Royce engine and Wilson transmission. However, closer inspection shows an enlarged turret, modified hull shape and improved ventilation for the engine, and an alloy sub-frame to reduce weight. However, this was offset by slightly thicker armour, so it was in fact about 5 cwt heavier than the Mark IIB.

Production was shared between Vickers and Royal Ordnance, with a total of 42 tanks built, some of which reputedly carried the bigger .50-cal Vickers gun instead of the .303-cal. Virtually all of these tanks were shipped out to the Middle East around 1935 to increase the strength of the 6th Battalion Royal Tank Corps. This unit was created in Egypt in 1932, unofficially at first, by the amalgamation of 3rd and 5th Armoured Car Companies, Royal Tank Corps. To begin with it was limited to two companies of rather tired medium tanks and Carden-Loyd Carriers. In the event, it was C Company that took 18 Light Tanks Mark III to Palestine in 1936. A few of these tanks were also operated by the Egyptian Army.

**B**

## 1. LIGHT TANK MARK III, EGYPTIAN ARMY

The Egyptian Army included a Light Tank Unit, which for a while was equipped with redundant British Light Tanks Mark III. It was extensively photographed for propaganda purposes early in the war, although the truth of the situation was somewhat different. Although it was under the command of senior British officers and reasonably well equipped with British weapons, the Egyptian Army was not comfortably disposed towards the British; it accepted joint responsibility for the defence of Egypt, without going to the lengths of declaring war, but was not entirely trusted by the British and was withdrawn from the front line when threatened. Relations between troops and their own Egyptian officers were not good.

The Light Tank Mark III dated from 1932 and was in essence an improved Mark II. Powered by a Rolls-Royce engine and running on the later pattern Horstmann suspension it was another two-man tank armed with a single Vickers machine gun and covered by slightly thicker armour. In pre-war years it was probably the dominant British light tank in the Middle East. It was used by 6th Battalion, Royal Tank Corps, in Palestine in 1936 and later by South African troops in East Africa, although it was not really suitable for a modern conflict. In Egyptian service the light tanks were painted a light stone colour overall, with limited Egyptian markings.

## 2. LIGHT TANK MARK IV, 102 OFFICER CADET TRAINING UNIT, SANDHURST, AUGUST 1940.

The 102nd Officer Cadet Training Unit (102 OCTU) was formed from the Westminster Dragoons (whose badge is illustrated) in the early part of the war. They did their training on a selection of light tanks, many of which were rather past their prime. This Light Tank Mark IV is typical; the last of the two-man light tanks, it dated from 1934 but was destined to be replaced by three-man light tanks fairly soon. Of an unusual shape which tends to give the impression that it was short in length and tall in height, when in fact it was neither, it still had an alarming habit of pitching forwards on rough ground; the tank commander was therefore provided with two hand grips on top of the turret to prevent him from being thrown out.

The tank is finished in a popular disruptive camouflage scheme of green and black but the broad white band, on the lower half of the turret, was introduced in the United Kingdom towards the end of 1940. The other prominent marking, the white circle and cross, was adopted and applied to vehicles taking the part of the enemy in a military exercise. Notice also the irregular patch of lime green painted on the sloping surface in front of the driver. This was gas-sensitive paint which would change colour in the presence of poison gas, prompting the crew to wear their gas masks if it was present.

**1**

**2**

TI 35-5

A Light Tank Mark IV following a Light Tank Mark VI over Wool Bridge near Bovington. The house on the left is Woolbridge Manor. This shows, better than a front view, how the turret was offset to the left, although the big bundle of canvas alongside the turret would make it difficult to rotate.

Yet that was not the end of the story of the Light Tank Mark III; their true moment of glory was still to come. In June 1940, 12 of these tanks, probably veterans of 6th Royal Tank Regiment, were sent from Egypt to Kenya and handed over to the South Africans, who operated them as No 1 Light Tank Company. Despite the fact that they had only limited training, the South Africans kept most of these tanks in service for the next 12 months, and they seem to have made an effective contribution to every battle they took part in. Most of the time they were carried on improvised tank transporters, which the South Africans called portees. Although South African military historian Commandant Neil Orpen described them as 'in appearance not unlike Bren-gun carriers fitted with turrets', they were certainly better than nothing, and achieved results out of all proportion to their numbers or effectiveness. Yet the Rolls-Royce engine gave evidence of excessive wear when used in a tank, so for the future it was decided to revert to a Meadows unit.

## LIGHT TANK MARK IV

The appearance of the Mark IV Light Tank in 1934 introduced a striking change in basic design. A lot of somewhat extravagant claims were made in respect of the new tank, mostly concerned with the construction of the hull, although it is difficult to confirm many of these. Even so it was an unusual design, unlikely to be mistaken for anything else. It was the last of the two-man light tanks to be built to War Office requirements, but it is not entirely clear what the designers were aiming for. At first sight it looks inherently unstable, with a tall hull and short track base. However, on closer examination these prove to be illusions. Much was made of the inherent strength of the hull, which in profile looks like a squashed parallelogram, interrupted only by the driver's hatch and the turret perched on top. Maximum armour thickness was 12mm and the overall weight was 4.3 tons. Even so, it is the suspension that creates the illusion: it looks shorter than on previous tanks because it lacks the rear idler wheel, which set a pattern for subsequent models. In fact in terms of track length in contact with the ground there is not a great deal in it. In respect of overall height it was lower than the later three-man types and only marginally taller than the Light Tank Mark II.

One change that looks like a reversion to earlier days was the return to the Meadows engine, the straight six type ESTE which developed just under 90bhp, giving the tank a top speed of 36mph. This made it the fastest of them all, and speed was going to be a vital factor for the future. The engine was located on the right of the hull with the driver sitting alongside it, while the turret was situated directly behind him, giving the tank a decidedly lopsided look, and making it very definitely left-hand drive. The Wilson pre-selector transmission was dropped in favour of a Vickers-Armstrongs five-speed crash type, and lever-operated clutch-and-brake steering. One can only imagine that this was a general return to simpler, more rugged systems that did not require so much careful attention and maintenance.

Nothing shows more how production of the Light Tank Mark IV was squeezed by previous and future models than the way its manufacture was limited to 28 tanks, 14 each from Vickers-Armstrongs and the Royal Ordnance Factory. This meant that the tank was never seen operating at battalion level. On the other hand they turned up everywhere, rarely in more than twos and threes but always very distinctive on account of their shape.

Although the two prototypes were designated as experimental Indian Pattern, they never went to India, and instead became prototypes of the Light Tank Mark IV. A third prototype, lacking any British designation, was delivered to India in 1933, where it was tested by the local authorities.

The Indian type can be easily identified by an upward extension of the turret, with a series of lookout flaps all around that served as a sort of cupola, something that was characteristic of tanks built for service in India. The armour on the Indian version of the Light Tank Mark IV was thinner, and the tank was known in India as the Light Tank Mark IVA. However, the tank did not appear in very large numbers because, as in Britain, a new model was in the offing. An original ledger gives a total of 29 and the date as March 1934.

An Indian Pattern Light Tank Mark IVA carries a flag-draped coffin during the funeral of Private Charles Floyd of 9th Light Tank Company, who died in 1937 from wounds received on the North-West Frontier. There was plenty of room alongside the turret to stow a coffin

# LIGHT TANK MARK V

One issue that had already arisen and been tackled at various levels was the growing awareness that a two-man tank was inadequate, certainly when it came to the role of the tank commander, who was also the gunner and wireless operator, as well as having a host of other, less tangible duties. Two Royal Tank Corps officers tackled the matter in a magazine article with the eye-catching title of 'The two-and-a-half-man light tank', although more realistically it soon became evident that anything less than a three-man tank would not be effective. As a result, the next two prototypes (L3E1 and L3E2) mounted larger turrets that could accommodate an extra man, and advantage was taken of the additional space to fit a second machine gun. This was a .50-cal Vickers gun, which at that time qualified as an anti-tank weapon.

The first prototype was fitted with a full-width turret, squared off at the back and flat on top, with what was known as a bishop's mitre cupola situated offset to the right on top. There is no evidence of a second hatch, and if the commander monopolised the cupola the gunner still had enough to do managing the guns. By 1939 the turret had been removed and the tank became the carrier/launcher vehicle for the prototype scissors bridge designed by a Royal Engineer officer and staff from the Experimental Bridging Establishment at Christchurch.

The second prototype, L3E2, had a different turret design, sloped at the back and with a drum-shaped cupola for the commander on the right. Alongside it on the left was a simple hatch for the third man so he could at least poke his head out and see what was going on. The turret, being larger and heavier than on the two-man tanks, was fitted with a crowded ball race to make it easier to traverse, and was secured by six brackets to prevent it from jumping off. The turret also included a rotating portion of the floor, which carried wireless batteries, ammunition containers and a seat for the gunner, attached to a stay, while the commander was provided with a rotating cupola so that he could survey the battlefield. Geared traverse was also available, as it had been for all the earlier light tanks, although one revolution of the handwheel shifted the turret by only three degrees. In this form it was clearly similar to the production tank, 22 of which were built, sufficient for one mixed tank battalion. Sources vary – some say that a dozen tanks were first delivered to 1st Tank Brigade and that technical experts from Vickers-Armstrongs accompanied the tanks and worked with the crews to remedy any faults quickly. However, other sources do not mention this and refer to nine tanks, some of which were returned to the manufacturers for improvement while others were shared out between various establishments for trials. There may be some truth in both accounts but it just goes to show how the facts can get twisted depending upon how they are presented.

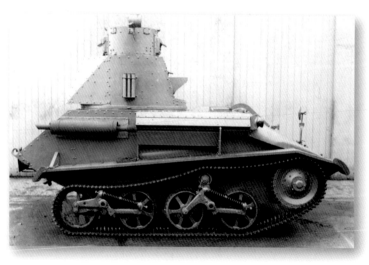

The special Light Tank Mark V built for India, of which there was only one. The machine guns have yet to be fitted, but the enormous cupola is readily visible with spotlight attached. The tubes on the side of the turret are for holding signal flags, but how anyone was supposed to reach them is not clear.

Three Mark V tanks of the 9th Queen's Royal Lancers (the queen in question being Queen Adelaide, wife of King William IV). The tanks look suitably immaculate and feature the regimental badge on the turret, but note how the turret slopes at the back, limiting interior space.

Another feature seen on some, but not all, production tanks was a pair of armoured air-intake louvres installed on top of the hinged engine cover plate. These may have been a later addition. In any case it is clear from photographs that most of these tanks were initially distributed to various newly mechanised cavalry regiments to help with training, so the chances that all 22 ended up with a mixed battalion seem highly unlikely. One Light Tank Mark V was modified by inserting an extra wheel station and having the drive sprocket moved forward. The idea seems to have been to extend the track base and improve stability in order to make it a better gun platform, but it was never developed.

## L4E1: THE SUPERINTENDENT OF DESIGN'S TANK

As we have seen, the design department at Woolwich Arsenal had been involved with detailed design and manufacture of some light tanks, but the basic features in every version were the responsibility of Vickers-Armstrongs, harking right back to the take-over of the Carden-Loyd company in 1928.

It therefore comes as quite a surprise to find the design of a new light tank awarded to the superintendent of design at Woolwich in 1936, and what is more that it should have been a three-man machine, which was then something of a novelty. One is forced to ask whether the War Office was giving Royal Ordnance an opportunity, or whether they were hoping to provoke Vickers-Armstrongs by presenting them with a rival. Despite many claims made for it in terms of originality and fighting ability, the basic design was little different from the Light Tank Mark V. New features included a rear escape door for the crew, an extended track base, an extra road wheel on each side and the reintroduction of an adjustable rear idler and armoured skirting plates covering the suspension. As a result the new tank turned out somewhat heavier. Although it served with 1st Tank Brigade in 1937 and was reported

The stretched Mark V with the extra wheel station and the drive sprocket shifted forwards, but without armament. According to the legend on the side, this peculiar tank also served with HQ 1st Tank Brigade.

The Royal Ordnance prototype L4E1 works up to a reasonable speed with a civilian driver. Even so it looks well protected, probably too well for its size, and although it served briefly with 1st Tank Brigade the type was never taken into service.

on favourably by the Mechanisation Board, it was never developed.

Mention should also be made of a series of light tanks built by Vickers-Armstrongs with commercial sales in mind. Since, by agreement, Vickers-Armstrongs were not permitted to use any features developed by the War Office authorities, these tanks were all slightly different from those issued to the British Army. Outwardly this seems to have applied only to the shape of the turret, but since matters such as armament and the type of radio fitted were left up to the customer, this also resulted in observable differences between tanks of the same type. Most of the countries that were customers for this type of tank were those that had no viable tank industry of their own, and Vickers-Armstrongs were competing with French, Italian and Czechoslovakian builders as well as Marmon-Herrington in the United States. Nevertheless, Britain's perceived pre-eminence as the first builder of tanks, along with the supposed expertise in their employment, still counted for a lot. Even so, it has to be said that the majority of light tanks supplied by Vickers-Armstrongs were no better armed or armoured than those used by British forces, and as such could not really be described as tanks capable of going into action against other tanks.

## THE LIGHT TANK MARK VI SERIES

The first of the Mark VI tanks, T1641, with its guns at maximum elevation. Note how the mud-encrusted return roller is attached to the leading bogie. This is one of the few really reliable identification features of this type, although the absence of raised cooling panels at the front is also an indicator.

It is tempting to see the Light Tank Mark VI as a version of the Light Tank Mark V with a new turret. It is probably more correct to say that they were all part of an evolutionary process. There were no prototypes as such this time, as there was no need, but from the first batch of 41 no less than ten went to MWEE for evaluation, and one of those was a very interesting tank. Tank T1667 was described as being fitted with a 2-pdr anti-tank turret. This was a fairly large turret, open at the top and fitted with a 40mm anti-tank gun. It was tested at MWEE and presumably rejected, although on what grounds is not known. It was a pity, on the face of it, because the time was coming, and it was not long away, when a light tank fitted with such a weapon would be very useful indeed. The other nine tanks sent to MWEE, and indeed the remaining 21 tanks in the batch, all appear to have been perfectly normal.

They had the same hull and suspension as the Light Tank Mark V, albeit with maximum armour thickness increased to 14mm and with the return rollers attached to the foremost bogie. This arrangement seems to have been

regarded as being responsible for an epidemic of track shedding, which was cured in later versions. The same Meadows engine and transmission and the same cooling arrangements were also employed. However, the spacing of the suspension units was altered slightly to give a better ride across country. The turret was different: inside it was provided with a fully rotating floor that carried the gunner and commander around with it, and externally it was extended and squared off at the back, not unlike the turret of L3E1 in this respect, in order to provide room for a No 7 wireless set. This gave rise to what might have been an awkward situation, which had first surfaced in the case of the Light Tank Mark V. The Royal Tank Corps wanted to introduce the position of gunner/operator, which had not existed before. They desired that the gunner should also be the wireless operator, rather than the commander, and it was necessary to negotiate with the trade unions before this could be permitted. These tanks were also seen with two 4in smoke-grenade dischargers, one fitted on either side of the turret, but since these were also found on the Light Tank Mark V tanks, they may have been a later fitting. The overall weight had increased to around 5 tons, but this had little effect upon the performance.

A Light Tank Mark VIA, finished in a most unusual camouflage scheme. The angular cupola is a clue to its identity, but most positive of all is the fact that the track return roller has been moved further back and is now fitted directly to the side of the hull.

A Light Tank Mark VIA fitted with the extended suspension intended to provide greater stability and a better gun platform. An extra double bogie has been fitted, reversed, at the back, and both bogies have additional shock absorbers and their own return roller. The turret has also been modified: the cupola has gone and been replaced by a low hatch complete with a periscope.

Three more batches of the Light Tank Mark VI followed for small numbers of tanks, two from Vickers-Armstrongs, but the third from the North British Locomotive Company, a large private company based in Glasgow. This was part of government policy to expand tank production into the private sector with war imminent, so that other engineering concerns would gain experience of tank production. Individual tanks were sent out to the Western Desert for evaluation under extreme conditions, and one, fully equipped with sand shields, was even photographed at Siwa Oasis, deep in the Egyptian Desert, which has legendary associations to the Oracle of Amon.

The next batch of tanks were classified Mark VIA, and were built in three batches amounting to 110 tanks in all, with one contract being awarded to the Royal Ordnance Factory. Three went to MWEE for evaluation while ten were sold to Australia.

Distinctive features of the Light Tank Mark VIA were that the return roller was now removed from the front bogie on each side and attached directly to the hull, and the commander's cupola was made more angular, becoming essentially octagonal in shape, with glazed lookout ports at the front. An improved version of the Meadows six-cylinder engine, type ESTB, was also fitted, although rated at the same horsepower.

An Indian Pattern Light Tank Mark VIB, easily identified by the lack of a turret cupola, photographed in Persia (now Iran) in October 1941. It was probably in service with the 14th/20th Hussars. By the time this photograph was taken the Shah of Iran had agreed to an armistice.

The next batch, the Mark VIB, was produced in substantial numbers and may be taken as the definitive version of the tank, though not the final one. In terms of appearance it retained the return roller on the hull side, was fitted with a drum-shaped cupola like the Mark VI, but this time with lookout windows, and had only one armoured louvre, the upper one, on the engine cover at the front. In other respects it was the same as the preceding models. Nearly 1,000 of these tanks were produced by a range of firms including

**C**

### 1: LIGHT TANK MARK V, 9th QUEEN'S ROYAL LANCERS

The Light Tank Mark V was the first three-man light tank to see service with the British Army, appearing in 1934. Production was limited since it was overshadowed by the improved Light Tank Mark VI. It was powered by a six-cylinder Meadows engine and armed with a pair of Vickers machine guns, one of .303-cal alongside a heavier weapon of .50-cal, which at the time was regarded as an effective anti-tank weapon for use against lighter vehicles. In practice, as it turned out, this gun was not even good enough to penetrate the armour of an enemy light tank.

The 9th Lancers mechanised shortly before the war, in 1937, disposing of most of their horses and adopting armoured vehicles instead. For the younger soldiers this was no hardship at all since they tended to find horses tiresome, but to the older soldiers, particularly the officers, it was a considerable wrench since it required the rapid adoption of new skills. In fact most cavalry regiments went first into armoured cars although the 9th Lancers seem to have specialised in tracked vehicles and field-tested many interesting prototypes. In typical cavalry fashion their vehicles were maintained to a very high standard, finished in gloss paint, which was quite unsuitable for war, with regimental insignia emblazoned on both sides of the turret. All armoured regiments were incorporated into the Royal Armoured Corps in 1939.

### 2. LIGHT TANK MARK VI, 2-pdr TANK DESTROYER

Good as it was mechanically, and available in vast numbers, the Light Tank Mark VI had one serious failing. It was not provided with an armament powerful enough to disable, let alone destroy an enemy tank – not even an enemy light tank, its own contemporary. Thus when it appeared in prototype form in 1935 the special version of the Light Mark VI, fitted with a 2-pdr (40mm) anti-tank gun in an open top turret, was seen as a very useful piece of equipment. It went to MWEE in about 1938 and was extensively field tested by the 9th Royal Lancers, but no production orders followed. It remained a unique piece of equipment.

Judged by appearances, since photographs are all we have to go on, the design seems to be quite well balanced. The turret mounting the 2-pdr gun was undoubtedly heavier than the normal machine-gun turret fitted to the tank, despite being open at the top, but it should have been possible to strengthen the rearmost suspension unit if required. As it was the design was rejected, possibly because it did not accord with British ideas on armoured reconnaissance at the time; it must be said that enemy light tanks were no better off in this respect, although they were somewhat better armoured. Even so it remains a most interesting and potentially useful prototype which could have proven very effective in the not-too-distant future.

1

2

A Light Tank Mark VIB, once used by the Canadian Army but latterly in the Ordnance Museum at Aberdeen Proving Ground in Maryland. It has since been removed for restoration. Features to note include the single ventilation panel over the engine, the drum-shaped cupola and the return roller bolted directly to the side of the hull.

the Vulcan Foundry, John Fowler & Co of Leeds, Ruston & Hornsby, Armstrong-Whitworth, North British Loco and Vickers-Armstrongs. In addition to seven supplied to Canada, some were supplied to Egypt and Turkey and one to Iraq.

The Indian Pattern Light Tank Mark VIB, a special version of the Light Tank Mark VI, was prepared for service in India. A contemporary ledger gives the total delivered as 93 with the date as 24 August 1936, which ties in closely with general production of the type but clashes with another claim quoted below. The tanks appear to have been identical to the British model except for the fact that on the Indian Pattern no cupola was fitted to the turret. It is not entirely clear why this was so, as hitherto a cupola was considered essential for light tanks in India, but now for the first time this fixture was no longer considered necessary, and instead the commander was provided with a periscope in his hatch. To begin with these tanks were issued to British light-tank companies in India, Royal Tank Corps formations that had grown out of earlier armoured-car companies, but when these were disbanded just before World War II the tanks were passed on to newly mechanised regiments of the Indian Cavalry and to British Cavalry regiments such as the 3rd Carabineers and the 14th/20th Hussars that were 'mechanised' in that country. Even so, there were never sufficient light tanks to go around.

Indian Pattern light tanks accompanied a Royal Armoured Corps regiment to Persia early in the war. They were used briefly against Japanese forces in Hong Kong and a few seem to have turned up in the Western Desert. Where these latter came from is difficult to determine. According to a history of Vickers Ltd by J. D. Scott, published in 1962, 'in 1938 Elswick completed the order for light tanks Mark VIB for India', so it seems the chances of any remaining in Britain were slim. Even so, one source suggests that some Light Tanks Mark VIB built in Britain, the final batch as it were, had the same modification: the removal of the cupola and its replacement by a second flush hatch. If that is true then such tanks, seen in the desert, might easily be mistaken for the Indian version. However, the history of the 14th/20th Hussars by Lieutenant-Colonel L. B. Oatts, published in 1973, states that 'any (tanks) in India that were in good condition were liable to be called in and shipped off to the Middle East.' It is also important to point out that when the 14th/20th Hussars went to Iraq and later Iran in 1941 they were equipped with a mixture of Indian Pattern Mark VIB Light Tanks and carriers with which they fought a number of successful actions.

A Mark VIB fitted with Straussler floats carefully enters the water on Mytchett Lake in Surrey. The floats were unwieldy things and a nuisance to transport, but they did keep the tank afloat, even if progress in the water was dismally slow since it relied on the action of the tracks.

Shortly before the war the British Army decided to replace the water-cooled Vickers machine guns in armoured vehicles with air-cooled Czech-designed Besa machine guns. Naturally this was easier to achieve on some tanks than on others, and in the case of the Light Tank Mark VI it was relatively straightforward. The scheme was to replace the .303-cal Vickers with a 7.92mm Besa and the .50-cal Vickers by a long-barrelled 15mm weapon. This new mark of light tank, the Mark VIC, also had a turret fitted without the commander's cupola. In that respect it was like the Indian Pattern tanks and featured a periscope in one half of the commander's turret hatch, which replaced the cupola. The fact that the conversion was relatively simple seems to be indicated by an order placed with the Vulcan Foundry in November 1937 for Mark VIBs, the last 40 of which were completed as Mark VIC. Mark VIB tanks from this batch could well have been built without cupolas, although at present we have no proof of this.

At least one Light Tank Mark VI was tested on Mytchett Lake near Aldershot, equipped with a pair of floats designed by the Hungarian engineer Nicholas Straussler. Known as Series 2 floats, they were substantial pontoons attached to the sides of the tank to keep it buoyant in the water. However, since the tank relied on the action of its tracks to propel it, progress would have been dreadfully slow. The plan was to issue these floats to divisional cavalry regiments on the scale of six pairs per regiment. Some 120 pairs were

A Light Tank Mark VIC is shown here, although with the turret turned away from the camera it is not easy to tell. The main reason for selecting this picture is because it shows a light tank fitted with the heavier two-piece tracks and the slightly larger double drive sprocket at the front. We are still seeking an official explanation for this.

## LIGHT TANK MARK VIB

The Light Mark VIB was the definitive version of the old Light Mark VI series. It was a three-man light tank, weighing a little over five tons, armed with a pair of machine-guns in a dual mounting: a Vickers water-cooled .303-cal on the left with, alongside it on the right, the larger .50-cal weapon. The driver sat low down on the left with the engine, a Meadows six-cylinder petrol unit, on his right, separated by a thin steel bulkhead. Most of the driver's controls were as normal; clutch, brake and accelerator pedals and a five-speed-and-reverse gear lever to his right. At the front, between his knees, were the two steering sticks. The radiator was situated above the engine, beneath an armoured cover but drawing air through a heavily protected ventilation louvre.

The Horstmann suspension gave a comfortable ride although it tended to be rather bouncy across country, making it impossible to fire at all effectively on the move. Normally the tank had to stop in order to aim and fire accurately. Two men occupied the turret: the commander on the right and his gunner to his left. The turret itself had manual geared traverse; elevation and depression, within limits, was controlled manually, and a tray was provided outside the turret at the front to catch discarded shell cases. A No 9 wireless set was installed on a shelf in the back of the turret and a rotating floor was provided that went around with the turret, carrying the crew with it. Smoke projector dischargers were fitted, one on each side outside the turret, and there was a spotlight ahead of the cupola on the front of the turret.

### Specifications

| Crew | 3 |
|---|---|
| Combat weight | 5.2 tons |
| Length | 12ft 11.5in |
| Width | 6ft 9in |
| Height | 7ft 3.5in |
| Engine | Meadows ESTB six-cylinder petrol, 88hp @2,800rpm |
| Transmission | five speed and reverse gearbox, clutch and brake steering |
| Fuel capacity | 30 gallons |
| Max speed | 35mph (on road) |
| Max range | 130 miles |
| Fuel consumption | 4mpg |
| Vertical obstacle climbed | 2ft |
| Gap crossed | 5ft |
| Armour thickness | 14mm (max), 4mm (min) |
| Armament | one Vickers .50-cal machine gun, one Vickers .303-cal machine gun (in dual mounting); two 4-inch smoke bomb dischargers |

## KEY

1. Rear idler/track adjuster
2. Shovel
3. Track
4. Jack
5. Road wheel
6. Suspension main spring
7. Return roller
8. Starting handle
9. Headlamp
10. Pyrene fire extinguisher
11. Drive sprocket
12. Steering levers
13. Engine firewall
14. Gear change lever

15. Lower driver's escape flap
16. Upper driver's escape flap and visor
17. Transmission cover
18. Radiator
19. Front towing/lifting eye
20. Rear view mirror
21. Armoured air intake (part of)
22. Air cleaner
23. Meadows engine
24. Water tank for radiator
25. Driver's seat
26. 4in smoke bomb discharger, left side
27. Empty shell case tray
28. Flash eliminator

29. Dual machine-gun mounting
30. .303-cal Vickers machine gun
31. .50-cal Vickers machine gun
32. Commander's spotlight
33. Commander's sighting vane
34. Half of cupola hatch cover
35. Commander's cupola
36. Wireless aerial
37. Wireless aerial base
38. Commander's seat
39. Gunner's seat
40. Rotating turret floor

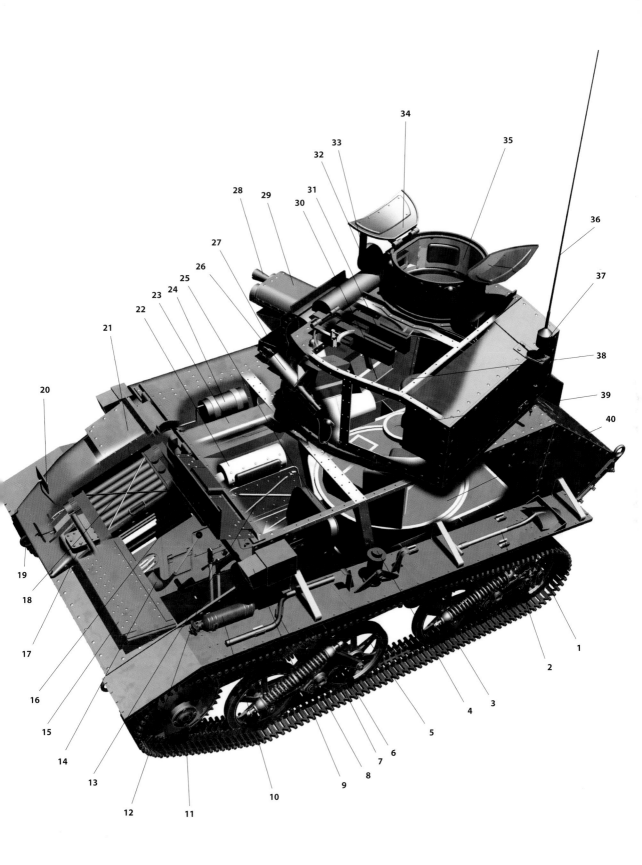

Light Tank Mark VIB Tanks undergo a full refurbishment inside the MG Cars works at Abingdon in Oxfordshire. MG undertook a number of these projects, including refurbishment of other tanks such as the A12 Matilda and full-scale conversions such as the Churchill AVRE and Centaur bulldozer.

The first of the Light Tank Mark VI anti-aircraft tanks, mounting twin 15mm Besa guns, which was produced experimentally at the Lulworth Gunnery School. This picture has often been printed the wrong way around and is invariably identified as a Light Tank Mark V.

made in all, but there is no evidence that they were ever used beyond this one time. The trouble was that the floats were quite bulky, so would have to be transported in a lorry and attached to a tank near to the water's edge, which was an unnecessary complication.

From about the middle of 1940 onwards, up to 100 Light Tank Mark VIs were 're-manufactured' by the MG Car Company works at Abingdon in Oxfordshire. This seems to have involved stripping them down and fitting new parts where necessary. The firm undertook similar work on Matilda infantry tanks. However, a claim that the light tanks were all survivors of the 1st Armoured Division expedition to France cannot be correct, since we know that only six of these tanks ever returned to Britain. One of the most interesting and so far unexplained modifications applied to Light Tanks Mark VIB and VIC concerned the tracks. These appear to have been changed to a double-link pattern, rather like a scaled-down version of the tracks fitted to A13 cruiser tanks. They appear to have been a bit wider than the original single-link tracks and required new, twin-ring sprockets, which are very distinctive. There is no reason to suppose that this was connected in any way with the work done by MG Cars and may even date from a while earlier. It is also difficult to see what difference it made to the tanks, apart from adding to the weight, and it was definitely not applied to all of them; the project seems to have ended, as it had begun, with little explanation or fanfare.

The final version of the Light Anti-Aircraft Tank was the Mark II, shown here with its gun turret reversed. The turret was armed with four 7.92mm Besa machine guns, but their limited range and restricted ammunition stowage meant that they were soon outclassed as aircraft flew faster and higher. They were converted from gun tanks, mainly the Light VIB version.

The idea that specialist anti-aircraft tanks would be required seems to have stemmed from experience in France, where the German Stuka divebomber first revealed itself to be a terrifying, if not actually very effective, weapon. This prompted Major-General Vyvyan Pope, the Royal Armoured Corps representative to the British Expeditionary Force, to advocate the conversion of light tanks to an anti-aircraft role. One tank, usually identified as a Light Tank Mark V but bearing all the hallmarks of a Light Tank Mark VIB, was converted at Lulworth Camp in Dorset to mount twin 15mm Besa machine guns in place of the turret, but mainstream production began with the conversion of a number of Light Tanks Mark VIA into Light AA Tanks Mark I, which involved raising the superstructure and fitting a shallow turret armed with four Besa 7.92mm machine guns. This was followed by a Mark II version of the Light Tank Mark VIB, which had a taller turret with the same armament but improved sighting arrangements. A total of 60 AA Tanks of both marks were produced and issued to headquarters squadrons of armoured regiments in Britain and the Middle East on the scale of four each. Whether they ever shot down an aeroplane is not so clear. The history of one of the newly created Royal Armoured Corps regiments, the 23rd Hussars, contains the following, telling phrase: 'we also received our first Anti-Aircraft Light Tank VIB which was not a popular vehicle.' This appears to have been towards the end of 1941.

A Light Tank Mark VIB of the 3rd Royal Tank Regiment photographed in Calais, probably after the Germans arrived. The divisional symbol of the British 1st Armoured Division is emblazoned on the front. It is very odd to see a Mark VIB here; one would expect it to be a Mark VIC. One wonders if this particular tank ever got into action at all.

The establishment of a light-tank regiment early in the war is typified by the 4th Queen's Own Hussars in Egypt in 1940. They were equipped with 52 tanks and a dozen Daimler Dingo scout cars. Of these, four light tanks were operated by regimental headquarters while the three squadrons had 16 tanks each. In each squadron four tanks operated with squadron headquarters and three were issued to each of the four troops; the squadron also had two Dingo scout cars and two motorcycles, the remaining

six Dingos being with regimental headquarters. When operating with a mixed formation that included Royal Artillery, at least one light tank was dedicated as an observation-post vehicle with a regimental driver and two Royal Artillery personnel in the turret. Mixed in with the fighting tanks, it was almost impossible to identify, and enabled the gunners to call down fire on any suitable target.

Incidentally, the 4th Hussars, who brought all their tanks out from England to Egypt, where they were unloaded at Port Said, say that before they could use them all tanks had to be fitted with, among other things, sand filters, sun compasses, sand shields and an extra leaf to the springs of each tank. They are the only regiment to mention this. Wartime activities in the Western Desert are recorded later.

The dismal performance of these light tanks and their obvious unsuitability for modern warfare may have had an unfortunate effect upon the career of the next light tank to be produced by Vickers-Armstrongs. The Light Tank Mark VII, or Tetrarch, never managed to establish itself in that role and, although perceived as a light cruiser tank on account of its armament, is really only famous for one event in World War II. On the evening of D-Day, 6 June 1944, eight Tetrarch light tanks of 6th Airborne Reconnaissance Regiment were landed by glider astride the Orne River, but only reinforced the point that a light tank has no place on a modern battlefield.

**E**

### 1. LIGHT TANK MARK VIA, 2nd LIGHT TANK COMPANY, AUSTRALIAN TANK CORPS, MELBOURNE

Australia took delivery of ten Light Tanks Mark VIA from Britain in 1937. They were a batch built initially for the British Army, so there were no concessions in the design for the hotter climate. Five each were allocated to the 1st Light Tank Company in New South Wales and to 2nd Light Tank Company in Victoria. Since these – along with four old and obsolete medium tanks – represented all the tanks in Australia at the time they were almost worked into the ground when Australia mobilised in 1939. Even so they were never used in action; Australian armoured regiments were issued with tanks, such as were available, when they went abroad.

The distinguishing features of the Mark VIA are the shape of the cupola and the double set of armoured ventilation louvres on the sloping engine cover at the front. This view is taken from a photograph of these tanks on parade in Melbourne; notice how, when the driver has opened up the front panels and his visor, the upper section almost masks the two machine guns in the turret. This is not as bad as it seems, since in action, when the guns are needed, these panels would be closed down. On each side of the turret there are metal brackets with slots in. These would normally support the smoke projector dischargers, although these were not fitted when the photograph was taken.

### 2. LIGHT TANK MARK VIB, CANADIAN ARMOURED CORPS, BORDEN, ONTARIO

Canada acquired 14 Light Tanks Mark VIB in 1939. They are said to be from an order originally proposed by Australia but subsequently cancelled. Again, like the Australian tanks, they seem to have performed adequately in extremes of climate, although in this case deep snow tended to clog up the running gear and the tracks. The Canadians established their centre of operations at Camp Borden, Ontario, at the time, commanded by the formidable Colonel F. F. Worthington.

The Canadian light tanks were identical to their British counterparts, with the same Meadows engine and Vickers machine-gun armament. Indeed, they even employed the same pattern of camouflage, only distinguished by their own rather limited style of markings. The tanks were not equipped with heaters of any kind but the crew were so squashed inside and so close to the engine that it probably did not matter much; wearing bulky clothing kept the cold at bay. The expansion of the Canadian armoured forces was slow to get under way but even so the shortage of tanks to train on was a severe hindrance. An influx of the American-built version of the Renault FT of 1917 helped, as did later tanks of indigenous Canadian construction, and this enabled Canada to field a substantial tank army later in the war.

1

2

## ON ACTIVE SERVICE

### The battle of France

Among the first units of the Royal Armoured Corps to arrive in France were seven light armoured reconnaissance regiments, each of which on full establishment should have been equipped with 28 Light Tanks Mark VIB and 44 scout carriers. They may have looked impressive to the British public, watching newsreels back home, but in reality they were almost completely useless, especially in view of what they were going to face in a few months' time. They were, in effect, the modern mechanised equivalent of the mounted divisional cavalry of earlier times; quite adequate for dealing with unarmoured troops but totally unsuitable for coping with enemy tanks.

Initially the armoured vehicles were shipped out and landed at Brest or St Nazaire in the west. Later it was found possible to go by the short sea route from Southampton. The story of all regiments is more or less the same, due to the nature of their equipment. The 15/19th Hussars explain that they had two sets of tracks for their tanks; battle tracks, which were relatively new, and training tracks, which were nearly worn out but used where possible to save wear and tear on the battle tracks. The position may be summed up by an account in the history of the 5th Royal Inniskilling Dragoon Guards:

A Squadron advanced to give battle but their (so-called) armour-piercing machine-guns had little effect on the German tanks and they were forced to give ground losing several vehicles and crews. It was becoming more obvious than ever how hopelessly inadequate were our fighting vehicles in the face

A French soldier has mounted this Light Tank Mark VIB to talk to the crew. Just ahead of him is one of the two 4in smoke-grenade dischargers fitted on either side of the turret. The top half of the driver's visor is wide open, obscuring the view of the tray for catching spent cartridge cases fitted underneath the guns.

of the opposition which now confronted us, German Panzers. The Mark VIB was not only thinly armoured but its suspension was so bad that across country it did not even have the advantage of speed. In this mobile armoured warfare the unfortunate Bren Carrier troops were in an even worse position, equipped as they were to do no more than hold ground against infantry and light vehicles – very light vehicles at that. In the whole regiment we could muster no weapon which could be sure of penetrating a German Panzer, and had to rely, in the situation now facing us, on bluff and quick thinking.

Their part in the adventure ended at Dunkirk at the end of May and early June 1940.

It should also be mentioned that members of Brigade Headquarters, 2nd Light Reconnaissance Brigade, formed a unit known as Cook's Light Tanks, using tanks drawn from an ordnance depot, as part of the special defensive force created to protect British General Headquarters at Arras. The only exception to this part of the story was 1st Lothian and Border Yeomanry, which was attached to 51st Highland Division. The division had been stationed further south, ahead of the Maginot Line with the French. As the German attack developed the division was withdrawn and, since there was no point in attempting to rejoin the original BEF, they were moved west to join British 1st Armoured Division west of the river Somme. By this time the German advance had really got into its stride, which the cruiser tanks of 1st Armoured Division were unable to halt. That being so, there was no hope at all that the light tanks of the Lothians would have any effect, and they were rapidly decimated, while the survivors fell back to St Valery and ultimately Le Havre.

Meanwhile the two regiments of 1st Army Tank Brigade, 4th and 7th Royal Tank Regiments, equipped mostly with Matilda infantry tanks, also operated about a dozen Light Tanks Mark VIB between them, which were used as headquarters and liaison vehicles. Second-Lieutenant Peter Vaux of 4th RTR has an amusing and telling story to tell of his experience during the battle of Arras on 21 May 1940:

A Light Tank Mark VIB from an unidentified regiment is seen crossing a temporary trench bridge. It sports the white–red–white national recognition sign in use at that time, on the front sandguard and on the side of the turret. The trigger mechanism on the smoke discharger has been shrouded, but the main armament seems to be ready for action.

I remember a silly thing that happened as we went back along that road. Some small anti-tank gun fired on my Light Tank and a shot went in through the left of my turret, just behind my gunner's head, and out through the right side of the turret just behind my head – I suppose we both turned a bit pale. Then, without a word, the gunner bent down, brought out his small pack, opened it and took out a very smelly pair of socks. He handed one to me; the other he stuffed into the hole on his side and I stuffed mine into the hole on my side! Somehow or other we felt much safer like that!

British 1st Armoured Division was landed in western France on 22/23 May 1940. It was supposed to move east and link up with the rest of the British Expeditionary Force across the river Somme, and was intended to consist of six tank regiments, mostly of cruiser tanks but with approximately 22 light tanks each. However, in the event only the 3rd Royal Tank Regiment got across the Somme. It was sent independently to Calais, where it was ultimately all but destroyed. However, shortly after arrival it did manage to send a light-tank patrol to St Omer, which, finding nothing there, returned to Calais. A few light tanks also took part in a breakout to Gravelines, although the majority seem to have been disabled protecting the port.

Meanwhile, further west, the remaining five armoured regiments of 1st Armoured Division advanced to the Somme only to find the Germans in possession and the area heavily defended. They were later joined by 1st Lothian & Border Yeomanry, one of the light armoured reconnaissance regiments then attached to 51st (Highland) Division, which fought until it was wiped out on the retreat to St Valery. Surviving histories of the division concentrate upon the activities of the cruiser tanks and the final event, in which

### 1. LIGHT TANK MARK VIC, HQ 2nd ARMOURED BRIGADE, 1st ARMOURED DIVISION, FRANCE 1940

The Light Tank Mark VIC was certainly the most distinctive of the tanks in the Light Mark VI series. This was due primarily to a change in armament which had been decided on shortly before the war. In essence it meant that Besa air-cooled machine guns should replace Vickers water-cooled weapons on all armoured vehicles; the 7.92mm in place of the .303-cal and the 15mm instead of the .50-cal. The 15mm, being that much longer than the .50-cal Vickers, was very distinctive. In practice the whiplash action of the 15mm limited it to firing single shots. The Mark VIC could also be identified by the lack of a cupola on top of the turret, flush hatches being provided instead.

In theory it was agreed that regiments of British 1st Armoured Division should be equipped with the new Mark VIC tanks while those of the divisional cavalry regiments should use the more common Mark VIB. In practice it did not work out like that. There were simply not enough Mark VICs to go around, so it seems that in the main those regiments of 2nd Armoured Brigade – The Bays, 9th Lancers and 10th Hussars – were the only ones to be equipped with this new type of tank.

### 2: LIGHT ANTI-AIRCRAFT TANK MARK I

Mounting four 7.92mm Besa machine guns in a small turret the Light Anti-Aircraft Tank was the first response to the German dive-bomber attacks that were experienced in France in 1940. In practice the relatively short range of the weapons and the difficulties of observing and tracking a fast-moving aircraft from a tank meant that it was almost impossible to shoot one down. There was only a limited amount of room in the turret, even without a tank commander, so a better-designed Mark II version soon appeared, although it was not much of an improvement.

Normal practice, when they were available, was to include four AA tanks with Regimental headquarters in an armoured regiment, but the vehicles themselves were never popular and when tests of the AA armament, which involved tracking a jeep with a can on the roof, proved too difficult, the entire scheme of basing AA vehicles on obsolete light tanks was abandoned.

**1**

**2**

light tanks are recorded as participating is the long-distance cross-country run by the surviving elements of 3rd Armoured Brigade, the RTR brigade, under Brigadier J. T. Crocker. A dozen light tanks, out of 14 that started, made it all the way to Cherbourg just ahead of the Germans. According to one source, the light tanks attached to 1st Armoured Division were of the Light Tank Mark VIC model whereas those with 1st Army Tank Brigade and the divisional cavalry regiments were Mark VIB. This would make sense, because many of the cruiser tanks with 1st Armoured Division were also armed with Besa guns, but it cannot be confirmed entirely, and some may have been Mark VIBs.

One other event of a warlike nature from around this time concerns the 3rd King's Own Hussars. On 6 May 1940, 17 men from this regiment with three light tanks were shipped to Norway from Leith on the Polish liner *Chobry*. They were originally destined for Harstad but the *Chobry* was diverted from there on the 14th, after landing most of its troops, and sent south towards Namsos with the men and tanks of the 3rd Hussars on board, along with 1st Battalion the Irish Guards. The ship was bombed relentlessly by the Germans and set on fire. The men were taken off by the Royal Navy escort, which then had to sink the blazing *Chobry*, which went to the bottom with the three tanks. Captain Tyrell, the officer commanding the 3rd Hussars detachment, wrote: 'What their story would have been had their tanks landed in a country where the only roads were precipitous goat tracks can only be conjectured.'

A few light tanks, reportedly six, had their suspensions modified to provide a steadier gun platform. This was done by fitting two double bogies on each side, facing back to back, with a separate idler wheel and two return rollers on each side and extra shock absorbers fitted to the suspension units. One at least was converted from a Mark VIA, while others are said to have

Any attempt to carry all the comforts of home on your tank was a tricky business, especially if one had only a Light Tank Mark VI. The stowage box and rack on the left trackguard was a standard fitting, as was the rack for extra fuel and water cans at the back, but there was nowhere to stow tents, groundsheets or bedding rolls; they had to be hung from the back as shown here.

A Light Tank Mark VIB in use as an armoured observation post by the Royal Artillery. It can be identified by the cable reel on the back, the chequerboard device on the side of the turret and the way the officer and NCO are scanning the battlefield.

been based on the VIB. In the case of the Mark VIA the turret was like the Indian Pattern, without a raised cupola but with a nearly flush hatch instead. Whether this was true of all the tanks so modified is not at all clear. It is said that this gave the tanks a much steadier gun platform but, as they found in France, the armament on these tanks was regarded as almost useless, so there was no point in the conversion. Some of these tanks are believed to have accompanied the 1st Armoured Division to France in 1940.

Any attempt to catalogue all the armoured regiments and other units in Great Britain that had Light Tank Mark VIs in the immediate post-Dunkirk period is almost certainly doomed to failure, and would probably include all of them, since the Light Tank Mark VI was by far the most common type of tank available. All we can hope to do is to concentrate on a few of the more interesting units and make some general points. For instance, before it was sent across to France in May 1940, the 1st Armoured Division, or at least the two brigades that would form it, were distinctly different, although seen as being complementary. In the original plan, 2nd Armoured Brigade, composed of three cavalry regiments, was designated as a light brigade to be equipped exclusively with light tanks, while 3rd Armoured Brigade, formed with three RTR regiments, was to be equipped with cruiser tanks. In the event, before they left for France the decision was taken to mix them up and create six regiments, each with a portion of cruiser tanks and the balance made up from light tanks, which were deemed to be ideal for reconnaissance, command and liaison duties. This was particularly hard on the cavalry regiments, whose men needed to learn the intricacies of the cruiser tanks very quickly to ensure that every regiment in the division had some tanks capable of fighting other tanks.

The British abandoned huge numbers of light tanks when they pulled out of France, along with many others. At first glance the light tanks would not appear to be a lot of use. The German models were better, and even they were regarded as something of a liability following combat experience in France. However, even the British light tanks had a workable and reliable chassis,

Major Alfred Becker is credited with this design, the le FH16, which used the hull of the Light Tank Mark VIB to carry a 105mm howitzer. Becker established a plant in France and built about 50 of these on captured British tanks. The armoured superstructure housed three members of the crew, behind the driver. The gun was an old one, more commonly seen on a two-wheeled carriage.

so a German officer stationed in France, Alfred Becker, initiated a comprehensive rework programme for local use. He came up with quite an effective AFV design with a built-up, open-topped superstructure mounting a French 105mm gun that could be operated by a crew of four. It went into such details as a pivoting earth anchor at the rear to provide stability when firing. There was even a command version with an enclosed superstructure surmounted by a small cupola. Classified as Pz Kpfw Mark VI(e) mit 105mm le FH16, it proved that although almost useless as a fighting tank, the Light Tank Mark VI could form the basis of a serviceable self-propelled gun – something the British might have been able to work out for themselves. Even so, the German conversions probably did not last very long, and seem to have remained in France on internal security duties.

After the fall of France, when the 1st Armoured Division was back in the United Kingdom, one of its armoured brigades, composed of just two regiments, could muster only 81 cruisers and 100 light tanks, although they

A pair of light tanks covering a road junction by a railway bridge during an anti-invasion exercise in southern Britain. The tanks belong to a mechanised cavalry regiment, which seems to have adopted playing-card symbols to distinguish individual squadrons.

were better off than the newly formed 2nd Armoured Division, which could manage only 178 light tanks, instead of the mixture of cruisers and light tanks it should have had on paper. This was probably typical for all regiments, those already formed and those newly forming, but it was unavoidable at the time and probably did not last very long, after more suitable tanks became available. On the other hand, Royal Armoured Corps training regiments seem to have retained some Light Tanks Mark VIB until 1942. The 51st Training Regiment based at Catterick certainly did, and probably the 56th at Bovington too. One retired officer, an NCO at the time, tells of how in the event of invasion he was expected to collect a Light Tank Mark VI from the driving and maintenance school, take it to the armoury to be armed and then to the wireless wing to collect a wireless set, before sallying forth to deal with the invading Germans. However, if we can base our information on photographic evidence then one of the biggest users of light tanks, even including some Mark IV tanks as well as Mark VIBs, was 102 Officer Cadet Training Unit, then a function of the Westminster Dragoons, which undertook extensive training in the Sandhurst, Blackbush area of Surrey.

Incidentally, some 50 light tanks, part of a commercial order by Vickers-Armstrongs for the Dutch Army, were still in Britain at the outbreak of war and were appropriated for the British Army. Designated officially as Mark IIIB, but known to all and sundry as 'Dutchmen', they were allocated for training. However, some of them, on the special instructions of the prime minister, were passed on for use by the Greek Army. All those that survived eventually ended up in second-line service with the German Army.

## The Mediterranean Theatre

Listing the regiments that operated the Light Tank Mark VI is almost pointless, and probably impossible. They include the tank battalions of army tank brigades, which had a handful attached to battalion and squadron headquarters of certain regiments such as the 3rd Hussars, the 4th Hussars and, initially at least, the 7th Hussars, which were equipped exclusively with light tanks. The majority of RAC regiments, at least in the first two years of the Desert War, seem to have been organised on a more generous basis as far as light tanks are concerned. Proportions up to about 50:50 appear to have been common, and that would apply to most of the regiments serving in that theatre at the time.

The 1st (Light) Battalion, Royal Tank Corps, was sent out to Egypt in October 1935 to add its strength to the tank forces already out there, limited as they were, during the Abyssinian crisis. They were equipped at the time with Light Tanks Mark VIA and remained out there until October 1936, to the detriment of tank brigade training in Britain for that year.

The battalion returned to Egypt in 1938, now equipped with Light Tanks Mark VIB complete to its establishment total of 52 tanks. It formed part of what was originally known as the Mobile Division (Egypt) but later became the famous 7th Armoured Division. It was formed under the command of Lieutenant-Colonel P. C. S. Hobart, but was initially woefully short of tanks.

Among the regiments already out there was the 7th Hussars. It had a selection of Light Tanks Mark III, Mark VIA and Mark VIB, but only sufficient to equip two squadrons; even then no heavy (.50-cal) machine-gun ammunition was available for the Light Tanks Mark VI, so they could only use their .303-cal machine guns.

The 7th Hussars was converted from horsed cavalry to a fully mechanised regiment after it arrived in Egypt, shortly before the war. It was issued with a mixture of light tanks, mostly of the Light Tank Mark VI variety. Its men make the point that the life of a tank in the Middle East was measured largely

Light Tanks Mark VIA of C Squadron, 1st Battalion, Royal Tank Corps, on outpost duty in the desert, just before the war. A Lewis gun is fitted, attached to a bracket on the commander's cupola. All weapons appear to have been covered to keep out sand, but the driver's hatches are wide open.

Abbassia Barracks, Egypt, and the 8th Hussars on parade with their Mark VIA light tanks just before the war. They were issued with badly worn tanks, previously used by the 6th Royal Tank Regiment and the 7th Hussars. Up to that time the 8th Hussars had been mounted in American Ford V8 pick-up trucks.

by the longevity of its tracks, and that since the tracks on most light tanks were very nearly worn out, they did not expect much of them. Once they had settled in and got used to their tanks they repeatedly heard rumours that heavier cruiser tanks would be arriving from Britain to replace them, but these remained only rumours for some time. When at last some did turn up, many without guns, the 7th Hussars received only enough to equip A Squadron to begin with. The other two squadrons went to war in their light tanks.

It has been said that when these light tanks were designed and first issued, the general belief in the British Army was that tanks were unlikely to fight other tanks, so machine guns and thin armour were considered perfectly acceptable. This assertion needs to be treated with care. Even back in the days of the old medium tanks, firing on the move was standard practice, and when the 2-pdr gun was introduced in 1936 it was almost exclusively for firing against other tanks. Of course, when the light tanks were first introduced they were seen as glorified armoured cars, and often used against forces that were not armed with tanks or vehicles of any sort at all. And of course, when the three-man light tank was introduced, from about 1935, its armament was improved by the addition of a .50-cal heavy machine gun because it was regarded in those days as a weapon capable of dealing with other light tanks and armoured cars.

The 7th Hussars took part in most of the early actions in the Western Desert, from the successful attack on Fort Capuzzo on 14 June 1940, to the assault on Tobruk in January 1941. In the former action they borrowed two Light Tanks Mark VIB, one each from 1st and 6th Royal Tank Regiments, the reason being that these tanks were fitted with powerful spotlights that were considered vital for use at night. They were also in the van on the difficult cross-country journey to Beda Fomm. The going was particularly unpleasant, with areas of slab rock and large boulders that reduced speed and increased petrol consumption to an alarming rate, not to mention the difficulty of negotiating areas strewn with Thermos bombs, which could damage tracks and suspension, albeit without harming the crew. The regiment arrived at Beda Fomm on 5 February and at once went onto the attack, capturing and destroying a number of Italian lorries.

Meanwhile, the 8th Hussars was making do, operating as a light car regiment equipped with American Ford V8 pick-up trucks, each armed with a single Vickers-Berthier light machine gun. The 8th Hussars, more fully the King's Royal Irish Hussars, started to receive light tanks early in 1939, or what they describe as cast-offs from the 7th Hussars and the 6th Royal Tank Regiment. These included seven Mark VIBs and 11 Mark IIIs, which were of course two-man light tanks armed with a single .303-cal machine gun, but by the end of April they had enough Mark VI light tanks to equip A and B Squadrons while C Squadron had to make do with the Mark III. Later still, however, C Squadron was rewarded with two troops of Light Tank Mark VI and two troops of the new A9 cruiser tanks.

However, just to prove that not all of the actions initiated by the British Army against the Italians were successful, it is necessary to recount a few details of the raid mounted by the 8th Hussars against the Italian camp at Maktila in October 1940. Maktila was the most northerly of a series of camps established by the Italians as part of their invasion of Egypt in the late summer of 1940. Indeed, Maktila was so far north it was virtually on the coast, and was occupied by the 1st Libyan Division of the Italian Army.

The attack on Maktila was mounted at night, on 23 October 1940, by the 8th Hussars and 2nd Battalion the Cameron Highlanders. Making a stealthy approach – the Camerons leading on foot backed up by the light tanks

A Light Tank Mark VIA follows a Daimler Dingo Scout Car through a gap in the wire into what looks like a tidily laid out British camp in the desert. The light tank appears to have its wireless aerial folded down in order to reduce its silhouette, but it carries no visible markings so it is impossible to tell the regiment to which it belongs.

One of the Mark VI tanks shattered by Italian artillery when it became bogged down in the salt marsh at Buq Buq. The 3rd Hussars lost the best part of a squadron here on 12 December 1940 when it impetuously attempted to follow up the Italian retreat by charging across unstable ground in the face of determined artillery fire.

of the 8th Hussars, which dared not come in too close for fear of suspected but unidentified minefields – the British were met by withering fire from every weapon the Italians could muster. The British attack had been anticipated, and the tanks and infantry had to withdraw. As dawn broke the 8th Hussars also came under attack from an armoured column of about 20 vehicles that emerged from the Italian camp at Tummar East, further south, and were unable to fight back since their tanks were cluttered up with Scottish infantry. They were obliged to withdraw, thankfully with no casualties.

The 3rd Hussars arrived in Egypt in September 1940, having come directly from Britain complete with their light tanks. Shortly after they landed, the regiment exchanged their B Squadron with the 2nd Royal Tank Regiment so that the 3rd Hussars had at least one squadron of cruiser tanks, albeit manned by 2nd Royal Tank Regiment. However, their first action saw the virtual destruction of one of their remaining light-tank squadrons. The light tanks had been directed against Italian positions near the coast following the battle of Sidi Barrani. A Squadron dashed forward in line ahead and swung into line abreast to attack the Italian position. Unfortunately, between them and the Italian defences lay an area of salt marsh, just to the west of Buq Buq. One after another the light tanks bogged down in the marsh, to be destroyed by the Italian guns. All told the regiment lost 13 tanks, the best part of a squadron, and the matter was not finally settled until the cruiser-tank squadron moved in and wiped out the guns. But by then it was too late for A Squadron.

Probably because there were so many of them, as much as for any other reason, Light Tanks Mark VIB turned up all over the place, although they were of palpably little use. Indeed, one even accompanied B Squadron, 4th Royal Tank Regiment, to Eritrea at the start of 1941. This squadron, otherwise equipped with 16 A12 Matilda tanks, was sent there to bolster an Indian infantry force that was attempting to defeat the Italian garrison. For the tanks it was as much a struggle against poor roads and rugged countryside as against the Italians, and although they were in action on a number of occasions they spent a lot of their time moving from place to place with great difficulty along mountain tracks that severely tested the transmission of the infantry tanks. For some reason they received 16 tons of spares for their one light tank and none at all for the Matildas, which they had to keep going by cannibalisation.

Winston Churchill's old regiment, the 4th Hussars, was sent to Greece as part of 1st Light Armoured Brigade Group. It was equipped exclusively with Light Tanks Mark VIB, while the other armoured regiment in the brigade group, the 3rd Royal Tank Regiment, was armed with cruisers. When the German attack began early in the morning of 6 April 1941 the armour was out in front, ready to receive them. But it soon became clear that the light tanks, armed only with machine guns, could not destroy German armour – they could delay them for a while by judicious use of ground, but not hold them up for ever. That required tanks or anti-tank guns, in both cases the hard-hitting 2-pdr weapon. To begin with the Germans could not tell whether it was light tanks, cruiser tanks or anti-tank guns that were firing, and treated all three with equal respect. However, once they had sorted out the sheep from the goats, as it were, and appreciated that the light tanks were virtually no threat to their armour, they dealt with them accordingly. In the end, however, it was the long and continual retreat with no time to halt for maintenance, over rough roads and tricky mountain passes, that wore out the tanks. By the time the 4th Hussars had crossed the Corinth Canal and proceeded by a roundabout route through the Peleponnese to the proposed embarkation port at Kalamata they were reduced to just ten tanks, which were soon bombed out of existence, leaving the survivors to fight on foot. By the end of April it was virtually all over – a number of crews got away, but the tanks, by now all wrecks, had to be left behind.

A short while later, on 11 May 1941, C Squadron, the 3rd Hussars, with 16 Light Tanks Mark VIB, was sent to bolster the defences of Crete. It was another forlorn hope for the 3rd Hussars, who were obliged to destroy all their surviving tanks by the end of the month, while the survivors escaped from the island as best they could. Nine A12 Matilda tanks of 7th RTR were also sent to Crete, but in the long run had little to show for their efforts and also had to be abandoned.

Malta, on the other hand, was a relatively peaceful location, if you overlook the air raids. At least there was no fighting on the ground. A variety of tanks were posted there at different times, including some Light Tanks Mark VIB and VIC, mostly operated by a troop from the Royal Tank Regiment that seems to have been known by a variety of titles. The most distinctive thing about the tanks on Malta was their camouflage scheme. It appears to have been a sort of 'crazy paving' pattern of brown lines painted over typical desert stone, intended to disguise the tanks against the background of dry stone walls that were a feature of the island.

Further east, a few light tanks were stationed for a time on the island of Cyprus. The force, which was equipped with Light

A Light Tank Mark VIB with all hatches open, which has come to grief off the road in Greece. It belonged to the 4th Hussars. The turret has been traversed to the rear and it is possible to make out the turret-mounted spotlight alongside the gun mantlet. The arm of service marking for 4th Hussars is the number 51 in white on a red square.

Tanks Mark VIB, Universal Carriers and 15cwt trucks carrying 2-pdr anti-tank guns was provided by the 7th Australian Divisional Cavalry Regiment, which had the difficult task, pending an expected German landing, of trying to simulate a much larger force by patrolling all over the island with crews wearing different hats. It was there from May until August 1941, after which the threat of invasion diminished. It was then transferred to Syria. Here it largely replaced the 6th Australian Divisional Cavalry Regiment, and encountered the 9th Australian Divisional Cavalry Regiment, similarly equipped with Light Tanks Mark VIB tanks and Universal Carriers, which had seen action against Vichy French forces equipped with Renault R35 tanks. Although relatively small, these were much better armed and armoured than the British light tanks, and in tank-versus-tank terms there was no contest. Even so, the Australians, by clever use of their equipment, ultimately managed to defeat the French forces and capture two of the Renault tanks in the process, which they proceeded to use against their former owners.

It seems that the 3rd Hussars were destined to be tied to their light tanks for years, and to be sent on some virtually suicidal missions with them. Following their attempted intervention in Norway in 1940 and their equally brave but ultimately pointless excursion to Crete in 1942, they were now destined to become involved in an even more fruitless attempt to save Singapore, in 1942. This time it was B Squadron, commanded by Major P. William-Powlett, which sailed from Egypt in January 1942. In fact they had reached Sumatra only two days before Singapore surrendered, and by the time they had unloaded their tanks and prepared them for action they were ordered to sail with them again for Java. This voyage was an epic in itself, since most of the tanks were loaded aboard a Dutch steamship while the balance of eight tanks had to be loaded onto a lighter and towed to Java

A tank finished in the exotic Maltese camouflage. This is a Mark VIC with two air-cooled Besa guns replacing the Vickers. It also features a turret without a cupola, but in every other respect is identical to a Mark VIB. The camouflage, which was supposed to disguise the tank against a local stone wall, features light stone-coloured paint, broken up into 'crazy paving' shapes with light-brown lines.

The 3rd Hussars again, this time with a Light Tank Mark VIB, photographed on the dockside in Java. There was not a lot that could be done with tanks such as this, but throwing them away on what we now know was such a futile expedition, and losing the men with them for the rest of the war, seems little short of insane.

by a tug. Even so they got there and unloaded their tanks at Batavia, where they undertook some tank training in the unfamiliar surroundings of jungle and paddy fields.

Following the disastrous battle of the Java Sea, Japanese forces invaded the island and B Squadron, the 3rd Hussars was incorporated into 'Blackforce', commanded by the Australian Brigadier Blackburn VC, and stationed at Buitenzorg. Blackforce, which included American artillerymen and Australian infantry, saw some action against the Japanese, but they later learned that the Dutch authorities had decided to surrender and thus ultimately, in obedience to orders, were obliged to deny their tanks to the invaders by pushing them off a mountain road into a deep ravine with a fast-flowing torrent at the bottom. None of the men escaped; all became prisoners of the Japanese. It was the end of fruitless adventures as far as the rest of the regiment was concerned.

## SUMMARY

In 1942 the retired soldier Vivian Loyd, once half of the erstwhile Carden-Loyd team, came up with his design for an air-portable light tank. It had many features of the earlier Vickers-Armstrongs light tanks, such as the suspension and front-mounted drive sprocket. The only difference was that it was right-hand drive, with the engine on the left, and apparently of an all-welded construction, but it was surmounted by the tiniest turret imaginable, capable of mounting only a single machine gun. Had Loyd really learned nothing over the intervening years? His tank attracted no interest from the authorities at all. At least they knew better, or rather had finally learnt something.

Vivian Loyd photographed with his prototype light tank, which he built at his own expense in 1942. What prompted him to do this is not obvious, but it was offered as an airborne light tank. What it might have achieved on the battlefield, armed with just one machine gun, is not at all clear.

In fact there was no place for light tanks armed only with machine guns in the armoury of a modern army, and probably never had been. For a country like Britain, with huge colonial responsibilities, often inhabited by truculent tribes, they had their uses, but that did not mean to say that they had any value at all in modern armoured warfare, as was soon made clear. If something could have been done, as indeed it was experimentally, to fit a more powerful anti-tank weapon to those tanks destined to fight in the west, it would at least have given them a chance, but sending them off to war with the same weapons used to subdue tribes on the North-West Frontier was akin to madness. The light tanks did have two things going for them: they were relatively cheap to produce, and they were fairly reliable. But since they carried no weapon more powerful than a heavy machine gun and were vulnerable to the most basic of anti-tank weapons, they were doomed.

Looked at from this distance, it seems as if the British were predisposed to start off on the wrong foot, due to their colonial heritage, but it has to be said that they learned quickly enough, albeit to begin with they were hampered by industrial limitations. Yet it is interesting to note that when a new light tank did appear, the Tetrarch in 1940, they seem to have been reluctant to employ it as such, and when first introduced to an American light tank in 1941 they initially classed it as a small cruiser.

The truth is that in the environment of armoured warfare the light tank will always be vulnerable, unless it can rely on its mobility, but if it is equipped with a respectable anti-tank weapon at least it has a chance. Those light tanks that equipped the British Army in France and later in the Western

Desert and elsewhere were entirely unsuitable for the role. They were the successors to a long line of light tanks developed in the insularity of harmless war games or in the unrealistic atmosphere of colonial policing, neither of which fitted them for combat in a real European war, when it came.

The idea that such tanks could have any part to play in post-war events seems to be ludicrous on the face of it, yet Britain, when it finally finished with the Light Tank Mark VI, passed most of them on to the Egyptian Army, possibly in the pious belief that they would be used only for training or perhaps for internal policing duties. But in this they seriously underestimated, as most people did, the impact of the creation of a Jewish homeland in the Middle East, the formation of the state of Israel and the virulent if disjointed Arab reaction to a lively Jewish settlement in their region.

As a result, when the Egyptian Army mobilised against Israel it did so with whatever tanks it had available: some Matildas and Valentines, a few Shermans and of course a quantity of Light Tanks Mark VI. At first they had to deal only with Jewish resistance groups armed with nothing better than improvised armoured lorries, against which even the Light Tank Mark VI had some potential, but with the creation of the state of Israel in May 1948, and the gradually increasing strength of the Israeli Defence Force with an equally heterogeneous collection of armoured vehicles, the Egyptian Light Tank Mark VI was really challenged. Even so, the Egyptians continued to deploy the type wherever they could until the early 1950s, when Britain undertook to modernise the Egyptian Army, and the old and useless light tanks were finally scrapped.

There seems to have been one final fling. At some stage the Israelis also acquired or captured a Light Tank Mark VIB, which they rearmed with a heavier automatic weapon. However, since it is widely accepted that one cannot make a silk purse out of a sow's ear, that tank, or what remains of it, is now found in the Israeli Armored Corps Memorial and Museum at Latrun. There are, in fact, quite a few surviving Mark VI tanks in different parts of the world, with at least one in Australia, one in Canada, two in the United States and two in Great Britain. They are worth a visit should anyone need reminding what these compact, strangely elegant and almost totally useless armoured fighting vehicles look like.

# BIBLIOGRAPHY

Barclay, C. N., *History of the 16th/5th The Queen's Royal Lancers 1922–1961*, Gale and Polden Ltd (1963).

Courage, G., *The History of 15/19 The King's Royal Hussars 1939–1945*, Gale and Polden Ltd (1949).

Fletcher, David, *Mechanised Force: British Tanks Between the Wars*, HMSO (1991).

Oatts, L. B., *Emperor's Chambermaids: The Story of the 14th/20th King's Hussars*, Ward Lock (1973).

Sellar, R. J. B., *The Fife and Forfar Yeomanry*, Blackwoods (1946).

Stirling, Major J. D. P., *The First and the Last: The Story of the 4th/7th Royal Dragoon Guards*, Art & Educational Publishers Ltd (1946).

White, B. T., *British Tanks and Fighting Vehicles 1914–1945*, Ian Allan (1970).

# INDEX